· · · · ·

"Val was prayer walking before anyone knew what to call it. During her prayer-filled walks around her local church campus, she sees glimpses of the Kingdom of God all around her. Her stories are an inspiration and an invitation to others to seek Him and to see His Kingdom here on earth."

—Janet Speer, Adult Leadership Consultant for the women's missions and ministries department of the Georgia Baptist Convention, SBC.

· · · · ·

PICKING UP PRAYERS

A NEW KIND OF PRAYER WALKING

PICKING
UP
PRAYERS

VALERIE BEESON-LYLES

TATE PUBLISHING & *Enterprises*

Published by Tate Publishing & Enterprises, LLC
127 E. Trade Center Terrace | Mustang, Oklahoma 73064 USA
1.888.361.9473 | www.tatepublishing.com

Tate Publishing is committed to excellence in the publishing industry. The company reflects the philosophy established by the founders, based on Psalm 68:11,
"The Lord gave the word and great was the company of those who published it."

Book design copyright © 2009 by Tate Publishing, LLC. All rights reserved.
Cover design by Melanie Harr-Hughes
Interior design by Stephanie Woloszyn

Published in the United States of America

ISBN: 978-1-60696-501-6
1. Religion / Christian Life / Prayer
2. Religion / Prayer
09.01.14

Dedication

• • • • • •

To my husband, Richard, I dedicate this book, my gift to you, as we celebrate our twenty-fifth wedding anniversary. You said it best, *Our love is real!* May God continue to bless and guide us during the next twenty-five!

Also to my daughters, Kaitlyn and Sarah, you are both beautiful and cherished gifts from God.

Acknowledgement

• • • • • • • • •

Give thanks to the LORD Almighty,
for the LORD is good;
His love endures forever.

Jeremiah 33:11

• • • • •

As it states in Jeremiah, Lord, I give You the praise
and thanks along with acknowledging Your amazing
goodness and love. Thank You for setting up the divine
appointments in my life to aid in accomplishing and
completing this book. May it inspire and motivate others
to glorify and honor You.

Thank You for Laura McKellar, and Dawn and Tim
Norton for challenging and giving me the confidence to
go after the dream of writing.

Thank You for my dear family, close friends, and church
body for encouraging and praying without ceasing.

Thank You for Melinda Harris for taking the time to
listen during her busy workday and for removing my final
excuse in getting this book written.

Thank You for Briarcliff Village's Panera Bread®, for
allowing this morning patron to "hog" a four top table

while savoring her Hazelnut coffee, studying the Word, and writing on this book.

Thank You for WordAuthority, Inc., for joining me for lunch after Susan McDaniel put us together and accepting the assignment to be my editor.

Thank You for Tate Publishing and Enterprises for seeing the vision that God has given to me contained in this book.

Contents

• • • • •

Foreword

• • • • •

People have been learning to pray since Jesus uttered those words found in Matthew 6:9, "This, then, is how you should pray." Now, Valerie Lyles teaches us a new way to pray in a manner that doesn't contradict His instruction but will inspire those who seek a deeper connection with their communities or busy women who like to multi-task.

She picks up trash and figures out the needs of her church by what she finds. Valerie, led by the Lord, describes how she discovered this method of praying and the ways it has blessed her and others. She provides step-by-step details for churches who want to start a prayer-walking ministry, and she expands the scope to businesses, homes, schools, and neighborhoods.

After reading Valerie's book, I began to pray in new ways while I was driving, jogging, flying, grocery shopping, and standing in line at the post office. Her sweet spirit and open mind will motivate you, too, to pray for people—especially those who don't know the Lord—in different and innovative ways. You may not want to pick up litter right now, but after reading this book, you will conclude that a little exercise and more prayer out on your walks will beautify your area, make you feel healthier and save the lost. What more could you ask for?

—Lorri Allen, "Mornings with Lorri & Larry."

Introduction

• • • • • •

It was August 2003, and our church needed a new pastor. Inspired by a book I was reading, I was determined to do my part to help the selection committee. The book was titled *Prayer Walk: Becoming a Woman of Prayer, Strength, and Discipline* by Janet Holm McHenry.

I decided to try prayer walking around our church campus. Prayer walking simply means you walk and pray at the same time. Ultimately, I ended up praying for much more than a new pastor.

On a Saturday morning while my family slept, I walked the three blocks from my home to Briarlake Baptist Church in Decatur, Georgia, near Atlanta. Heading to the back of our campus where the youth building, gym, and activities field are located, I immediately started praying for every aspect of the young people's lives—for the teachers in their final preparation of Sunday's lesson and for the students to apply the lesson to their lives. Walking toward the activities field, I prayed for the many children's soccer games that would be played that day, asking God to let all the kids have fun and safe games while learning good sportsmanship. I also prayed for the coaches to have opportunities to share the story of Jesus with the players. I lifted the activities staff in prayer—with its many responsibilities, including organizing the events. I thanked God for this area of campus that touches so many lives within our community.

Turning and walking toward the main group of buildings, I prayed for the children's area. Remembering what an impact the teachers had on my two girls, I prayed for the message of Jesus' love to penetrate the young hearts of all the kids who would be attending Sunday school the next day. Working my way down to the church library, I prayed for the volunteers who give their time, for the community that uses the library, and for the full-time staff who maintains it.

Next, the church offices brought to mind our interim minister. I prayed for his preparation for the Sunday worship service. I prayed for our staff and asked God to guide the pastor search committee. Moving to the front of the church, I looked through the sanctuary windows and continued praying for the music director, the choir, and the orchestra. "God, let Your glory be heard through the joining of voices and instruments," I prayed. At the adult classrooms, again, I lifted up the teachers' preparation and the class members' application.

On my final leg of the prayer walk, I happened to look down into a drainage ditch that separates our church parking lot from the street. I noticed with the distaste of an interior designer an abundance of litter. I thought, *Someone really needs to get down in there and clean that out before tomorrow.*

I heard a small, quiet voice suggest that the *someone* should be me.

"Not me! Lord, You know I don't clean my own home. And even at the office, I hire subcontractors to handle physical labor. It's my job to choose lovely fabrics, perfect colors, and beautiful accessories…not to pick up trash."

I looked at my watch, thinking I didn't have time for this. But I still felt a nudging.

"Me? Lord, are You sure?"

Even though I didn't seem like the best-suited person for the job, I wanted to obey. So, I carefully stepped down into the drainage ditch. I saw broken beer bottles, crinkled cigarette cartons, discarded tissues, batteries, and fast food lids still with their straws.

"How am I supposed to pick up and carry all of this litter?" I asked God.

Glancing ahead, I saw no more than two feet in front of me, a never-been-used plastic grocery bag. Grinning and looking up, I said, "Thank You!"

I picked the bag up and started my unexpected Saturday task. As I filled the bag, I then heard again that small, quiet voice saying, "Here…right *here*…are the needed prayers within the church."

It was as though the voice was telling me the litter represented the hurts and sorrows that people were hiding. The broken glass and the discarded tissue prompted me to pray for the broken lives caused by divorce, illness, job loss, or death. The cigarette cartons led me to pray for those who needed to break destructive habits and addictions. The old batteries inspired me to pray for lives burned out from long hours of work or uncontrolled circumstances.

Combing through the ditch, I noticed items caught between rocks and dirt. Tugging to pull them free, I prayed for the traps of life and those who wonder, *How did I get myself into this situation?*

Faded labels and mud covering the litter indicated it had been there for a long time. How many times in my own life have I let sin lie unconfessed hoping it will be hidden far from view and unseen by others? I realized that we get so used to the half-buried sins that we continue to walk or drive right past them, hoping they will just go away.

As I put the last piece of broken glass in the plastic bag, I realized the sack was the exact size needed to complete the job. Walking to the closest trash can, I felt reminded as I dropped the bag into it, that just as the bag was big enough to handle all the litter, the grace of Jesus is big enough to handle all my sin. I simply have to place the refuse of my life in an imaginary bag, give it to Him, ask for forgiveness and renewal, and then, let Him throw the sack away. The important part to remember is to not pull it back out of the trash and wade through it. A song I used to sing in my early twenties says it best, "Give it all to Jesus." The song does not say, "Give and take back."

Now on Saturdays, I head toward my church to pray for its people, its activities, and the upcoming worship services. While the rest of my family is still asleep, I grab a plastic grocery bag in anticipation of the prayer needs that the small, quiet voice has assigned to me.

Create in me a clean heart, O God, and renew a steadfast spirit within me.

Psalm 51:10

As you read this book, it's my prayer not that you pick up trash (although it is fine if you do), but that you consider new ways to pray for those you know and those you don't.

And if you find yourself near Atlanta on a Saturday morning, let's prayer walk together, I'll bring the bag.

It's All About Them:

• • • • • • • • • • •

TAKING PRAYER
TO THE NEXT LEVEL

Prayer walkers have a secret. They've learned to pray for people they have never met. Oh sure, we've all prayed for some we don't know, such as military personnel. And for generations, we've prayed for missionaries in foreign countries. Prayer walking becomes more specific, yet still petitions the Lord on behalf of unknown people.

Listen to a prayer walker:

Dear God, please bless the people in this house. I don't know them, but You know their hurts, fears and needs.

Lord, guide the leaders of this business so that they will make ethical decisions that impact the community for good.

Father, help the teenagers in this youth program come to know You better and commit their lives to You.

When we become burdened to pray for those we don't know, we move beyond a circle of family and friends and begin to live the biblical mandate of the Good Samaritan—that anyone who needs us is our neighbor and worthy of prayer.

When we "pick up" prayers by gathering trash, we learn to hear what—or who—God is nudging us to care about. Through the items, He whispers, "It may look like garbage, but look deeper. This is important to Me."

And when we see the picked-up prayers answered, we're thrilled, seeing the impact on our church, our family, our community, and our schools.

You might be thinking, *I'm a good pray-er but not much of a walker. Do I really have to walk?*

If physical limitations keep you from walking, think creatively. Maybe you can prayer golf-cart or prayer ride in the car. Or maybe you can pray over the church announcements in a new way, like I learned to, with the help of technology.

Technology has impacted my church, taking it to a new level of communication. We now have screens in the front and upgraded sound systems in the back of our two worship centers/sanctuaries, along with TV monitors in the public areas such as the corridors and dining hall. The large monitors not only serve members when the church is open, but when it's closed, too. This is possible because three of the monitors can be viewed from outside each of the glass doors.

Every Saturday during my prayer walk, I stand outside one of those doors and read all the items that scroll over the screen. They influence how I pray. I can still remember how excited I became reading the news that our new pastor's baby had arrived. The monitor revealed his name—Bailey—along with his birth date and his weight. I immediately prayed for this new precious gift that God had given our pastor's family.

Sermon topics also scroll across the display. They remind me to pray for the preacher and his sermon preparation. I also pray for those hearing the message.

Many of the church's activities are on the monitor. Each season, the sign-ups for different sports are listed. I pray for the upcoming season, for the coaches, chaplains, and players. Praying that God will be present in the practices and during the games, I ask for opportunities for the gospel to be presented not only to players but also to their parents.

In addition, the monitor shows the names of new members. I rejoice when someone has acknowledged Jesus as the Lord and Savior of his or her life. It's the most important decision a person can make. The monitors give me more ideas for prayers: mission trips, youth camps, women's events, and Bible studies.

• • • • •

Prayer:

Precious Father, thank You for the gift of technology that jogs our thoughts about who and what to pray for. Thanks for the nudges and whispers You give us to help us pray. In Jesus' name, amen.

Miracles in the Mess:

• • • • • • • • • • • •

DOUBLE BLESSINGS

When I first told a woman about my trash ministry, she looked at me as if I'd just stepped off an alien spaceship or I needed long-term therapy. But I was so blessed by picking up prayers that I knew I had to share my experiences, no matter what she thought.

That's why I urge you to prayer walk. Not only will you bless those whom you pray for, you will be blessed yourself, as I was the morning I picked up trash in a flowerbed. Catching sight of a clear piece of plastic and brown glass almost completely buried underneath dirt and pine straw, I was puzzled. I immediately recognized the beer bottle, but I had no idea what the plastic could be. Pulling it out of the dirt, I saw that it was a student driver's identification card. I didn't recognize the name on it.

While holding the two objects in my hands, I prayed for this young man and his driving skills. I prayed that he'd learn to be a safe driver. I prayed for God's protection to surround him so that he would have the wisdom to not drink and drive.

Because I didn't recognize his name as someone from

our church, I also prayed for his relationship with Christ. Instead of throwing the ID away, I saved it. When I got home, I placed it in my prayer-walking box along with the other items collected over the years.

Later, with the support and encouragement of our new pastor, my church formed a prayer team. During one of the first meetings, the co-chair asked me to tell about my prayer–walking experience. After I shared my testimony, I closed with a few examples of the saved pieces of trash and how they inspired me to pray. The student driver's ID was one item I talked about that afternoon. At a break, a deacon walked up to me, put his arm around my shoulder and asked if I knew the young man whose name was on the ID. I told him no.

Still with his arm around my shoulder, Mark asked if I'd heard about an accident three weeks earlier. It had closed down Interstate 85 north for several hours. I told him yes, I'd heard about it on the radio and had purposely avoided that area.

As Mark continued, I held my breath; it had been a fatality accident. The young man whose student driver card I held had been involved in it. He survived with only sustaining minor injuries. Mark worked with teenagers on Wednesday nights, and occasionally, the boy attended.

My knees weakened and chills covered my body. I asked in a silent prayer, "Lord, could this be correct? Could the prayers of a Saturday morning prayer walker make such a difference?"

This experience changed my view of prayer. I realized that God does not forget our prayers even when we have.

Had my prayer made a difference for that young man? God is the only one who knows. But His protection of this young man made a difference in my life and in my anticipation and excitement about prayer.

• • • • •

Prayer:

Heavenly Father, I praise You. Lord, thank You for answering prayer. Help me to never forget or doubt the power of prayer. In Jesus' name, amen.

Success in the Mess:

• • • • • • • • • • •

LEARNING TO LOVE LITTER

A designer by profession, I find fulfillment in artfully arranged rooms, colorful walls, the perfectly placed vase, and fabrics whose textures invite you to touch them.

So, learning to work with floor plans and creating interior spaces through finishes and furnishings makes plenty of sense. But learning to work with garbage does not. It's the last thing I would ever have imagined doing when I began prayer walking. However, these days, I look forward to what each week's trash haul will lead me to pray about as much as I do opening a new design magazine. It's the amazing stories of answered prayers that keep me walking, praying, picking up trash, and, yes, loving litter. It all started one day when I definitely *did not* love what I saw.

My eyes kept falling on an area in the middle of the parking lot filled with shattered glass. "Surely, Lord, You don't want *me* to pick that up," I pleaded.

Getting closer and seeing the thousands of tiny pieces of glass, I thought, *This will take hours to pick up by hand, and it's dangerous. I could cut myself.* "Lord, did You think of that? I really could cut myself. You wouldn't want that to happen, would You?"

With that excellent excuse, I walked to the playground, picked up trash, and put all of the toys back in place. I also prayed for the children who would play there on Sunday. When I emptied the bag into the trashcan, I saw it, a broom.

No, not a broom, I thought. "Lord, how did You know I would need a broom? This is not funny, God. Okay, I'll be honest. I'm not in the mood. I don't want to pick up the broken glass. There I said it. I don't want to."

The playground had been the final place I'd planned on going that day. I wanted to get home to fix breakfast for my family. That was just one reason, or should I say excuse, that I didn't want to sweep up the glass. Another reason I didn't want to do what I felt God calling me to do could've been that the task would involve a lot of bending. Because of a bad back, I need to bend at the knees to get low to the ground, and this clean-up effort would involve a lot of bending. I just didn't feel like putting out that much effort. However, I could think of many things to pray for looking at the shards of glass: shattered lives, broken hearts, and crushed spirits.

However, none of those was what this was all about. It was deeper, more personal. I began to walk home but couldn't get far. Turning around, I went back, picked up the broom, and pulled a piece of cardboard out of the trash to use as a dustpan. I knew the cardboard was there because I had put it in the dumpster earlier. It took a little while, but eventually, I gathered all of the broken glass. When I threw the last of it away, I put the broom back where I'd found it and the cardboard back in the trashcan.

"What was that all about?" I asked God again on the way home. Because I didn't pray for anyone or anything as I swept up the broken glass, I wondered why I felt led to finish such a distasteful task. The word "obedience" came to me. Picking up this undesirable litter was about being obedient even when I didn't understand why. The significance of being obedient came to mean so much when a prayer I had for the church was answered in an obvious, beautiful way.

A courtyard sits in the middle of several church buildings. On a bench I would often rest and think about the church's teenagers and the out-of-state mission trips they had taken over the years to help others with their homes and yards. So I started praying, "Lord, could our teens work one weekend on their home church?"

Every week for a year, I prayed for our youth to work on the landscaping.

One Saturday morning, I turned down the sidewalk leading to the courtyard. A habit now, I prayed for the youth group to help with the landscaping. As I stepped into the courtyard, I couldn't believe my eyes. Brand new sod, flowerbeds, decorative rocks, and ferns brought much-needed beauty to the area. *How did this happen?* I couldn't help but think God was just waiting to see the shocked expression on my face! Here before me was an answer to prayer. I fell to my knees to feel the fresh sod beneath my feet and to thank God. Then I wondered, *Who had done this, and when did they do it?*

It wasn't until a couple of weeks later that I overheard some of the students in my ninth grade Sunday school class say that they'd helped a member of our church with landscaping. That word captured my attention, so I asked for more about the story. One of the boys said Mr. Cosby, co-owner of Falling Leaves, a local landscape company, felt led by God to gather several youth volunteers to landscape the courtyard.

After Sunday school, I located Allen Cosby and asked him about the courtyard. He confirmed that he had indeed felt led to do something about that place between the buildings. Both he and the young people enjoyed hearing that I had been praying for that area. Now I'm praying for several adult Sunday school classes to take an area and landscape away! This experience has taught me the power of prayer. I didn't say a thing to anyone about it, and God handled the rest.

Another Saturday, toward the end of my walk, I noticed a small, crumpled piece of paper lying on the sidewalk near a set of double doors. It had three words written on it:

Out of order

My immediate response was, "Please Lord, *no!* Please don't let this happen to the church."

Yet, I realized I should be asking God, is there an area in the life of the church—or in my own life—that may be going in that direction? Are people or practices *out of order?* Do we need help in getting back on track or back in working condition? So, I asked God to reveal what was not functioning properly according to His perfect plan. In looking back at the piece of paper, I concluded it was a note that had fallen off an appliance like a broken coffee pot or CD player. The handwriting looked like my grandmother's, so I felt the elderly lady who'd likely written the note would never have dreamed how it impacted my thoughts and motivated me to pray.

Now, do you see why I love litter? With it comes life-changing prods and prayers. I encourage you to pick up prayers among the trash, too.

• • • • •

Prayer:

Our Father, I come to You in an honest and humble way. Start with me first. Show me the areas in my life that are out of order or off balance. Help me not to be afraid and to have the courage, on a daily basis, to ask You for instructions on where I need to grow and go. Keep me focused on the path You have set before me. Thank You, Lord, that You have a purpose and a plan for me and my church family. In Your Son's name, amen.

Walking and Talking:

• • • • • • • • • • •

HOW TO PRAYER WALK

Jesus tells us to pray without ceasing. Prayer walking is a way to bring prayer into our daily activities by having a nonstop conversation with God about everything. It's not possible to enter into these talks without becoming more sensitive to others, without being more cognizant of one's own blessings or without developing more dependency on Him.

There's another aspect to this practice that's powerful: God can use us as tools anywhere, anytime. Prayer walking allows us to be an active part of God's plan in a way that's different from the role of the traditional teacher or preacher.

More About My Prayer Walking Journey

Maria Manahan always asks for prayer for others over and above asking for prayers for herself. One night at Bible study, she asked for prayer for the pastoral search committee. I tucked away her prayer concern for later.

Two nights that week, I had stayed up reading a new book on prayer walking. With only a few pages left,

Sunday morning rolled around. During the beginning of the service, the chairman of the pastoral search committee presented a report. He shared the group's progress and said how much he appreciated the support and prayers of the church. I thought of Maria and once again wondered what I could do to help with this process.

During the service, I started praying about it. The new book I was reading came to mind, particularly a chapter about the author praying for her church one day a week. So, I planned the next Saturday to prayer walk, not expecting or even anticipating what would occur during the time.

As I mentioned in chapter two, after I began prayer walking and picking up trash, I wanted to share with others at the church what God was showing me each Saturday. That next Wednesday night, the opportunity came up; I jumped at the chance to tell about prayer walking.

However, the response was not what I expected. After talking about my first "trash time experience" and how God shared what the true prayers of the church were, I got the response of rolled eyes and the comment, "Aren't you creative?"

Although discouraged, I told God, "I'm not quitting, but I am not going to tell another soul about this."

Prayer walking quickly became one of my favorite times during the week. It was addictive to hear from God and feel so close to Him. I began to hear rumors that the pastoral search committee had found God's new leader for our church. Soon after on a Saturday morning,

I turned the corner and saw many vehicles in the staff parking lot. I instantly recognized two of the vans parked in the lot as belonging to my friends Irene Simoneaux and Carol Snyder. They were on the search committee. Overwhelmed, I had to stop and pray. I literally flattened myself up against the brick wall underneath the second floor window of the conference room. I felt sure the committee was meeting in there. I didn't want to be seen or interrupt the meeting. I couldn't help but wonder, *Is the prospective pastor in there with them, or is the committee alone?* Either way, I prayed for God to give them wisdom in this important decision that would affect the future of our church.

Later that day, I saw Irene and asked her about the meeting. All she could share with me was that an announcement would be made during the Sunday service. She asked what I was doing there, so I told her about my prayer walking experience and was relieved that she was encouraged by it.

Sunday the announcement came, and sure enough, we had a new pastor. What a time to rejoice! God had answered our prayers. After Dr. Tommy Ferrell came on board, Irene shared with him that a woman had been prayer walking for close to two years for the church and for the pastor search. Through a series of events, he discovered who I was, and I was able to tell him my picking-up-prayers story. He was touched by it and encouraged me to continue this ministry. Later, he invited me to co-chair the newly formed prayer team committee. Never had I been so excited to be on a church committee.

David Terry, the chairman, asked me to give a devotional to open the meeting. The upcoming Prayer Walk was the main agenda item. After hearing my story, Tommy, the new pastor, asked me to give my testimony during the Sunday morning church services to motivate people to come to Briarlake Baptist's first Prayer Walk. I instantly panicked, praying, "God, he doesn't know what he is asking me to do. I can't stand up in front of the church to only be laughed at because of the 'creative' way You inspired me to pray."

But Tommy insisted, and not wanting to disappoint him, I agreed to do it. I had to shake my head and pray. "Lord, You know how much I have wanted to speak, but this isn't the topic I thought I would be speaking on. I thought it would be about the importance of Bible study."

I went home after that meeting and told Richard, my husband, that we might be asked to look for another church to attend. There was one more reason I agreed to talk about prayer walking. A few months earlier during one of my Saturday prayer walks, I got a vision of one hundred church members walking, praying, and singing together the song "We are One in the Spirit."

Tommy called me the week before I was to give my prayer walking testimony to tell me that the service was full, and I had only three minutes. But he knew I couldn't say anything in three minutes, so he was giving me five! To myself I thought, *Five! How can I do it in five?*

I practiced all week in the car, in my office, during cleanup time after dinner. I started out at twenty minutes and then got it down to ten minutes. Finally, after feeling as if I was cutting most of the meat out, the speech was just five minutes. That morning, I was so nervous that I prayed constantly. I took the advice of a friend, Janet Speer, who speaks often. She suggested that I write out my speech, take it up with me, begin, and walk away. Let the Holy Spirit lead from that moment. So....that was what I did. God was faithful, and He did take over. I'm not sure how long I actually spoke, but I didn't get pulled off the platform, so I thought that was good. As I started speaking, and especially when I started talking about the trash in the ditch, I could feel all ears listening and saw some tears flowing. After I finished, I sat down and felt like crying myself. I prayed, "Lord, You did it, but did they get it?"

The response was overwhelming. Before I spoke, only two people were signed up for the Prayer Walk, and that next Saturday seventy showed up! It was an amazing time for all. God worked in lives in different ways—renewal for some, confession for others, recognition, and confirmation of the power of prayer for everyone who participated.

Think Creatively

Prayer walking makes it no longer possible to sit on the sidelines and say, "I can't be involved." No excuses fly. Because prayer walking works even if you're running, standing, sitting, driving, flying, riding, sailing, skating, strolling, watching, wading, fishing, working, or surfing.

You can even look at a map and pray for the people of a foreign country or look at your calendar and pray for opportunities to serve.

Prayer walking is a challenge to be an active player in God's grand plan to touch others—and the world.

A Prayer-Walking Journal

When you return from your walk, you might want to keep track of what you prayed for and then later see how your prayers were answered. You won't always know the results of your prayers, but sometimes God will let you know He has heard you. Here's an excerpt from my prayer journal.

June 25, 2005

- Picked up beach toys, shovel, and sifter. Placed back in sandbox. Prayed God would help us all to dig and sift through His Word for the truth. Thought about how children play for hours in the sand and prayed we all spend hours in the Word and meditation.

- Evelyn drove by and spoke to me. She shared about the Angel Food Ministry. Also that she and Chris were adopting a girl from China. She asked me to pray for the child's health and their preparation.

- Prayed for the wedding that was taking place in the church later.

- Prayed for the July 3 event.

- Prayed for the new sound system being purchased for the Backlot worship center.

- It was a beautiful morning. Birds were singing and the breeze was gentle.

- Prayed for the youth on their trip to Muncie, safety and learning in the process of helping. Changed lives for Jesus!

July 2, 2005

- Prayed for the July 3 event.

- Safe travels for the youth returning from World Changers.

- Susie drove by, going to office. Prayed for her.

- Found several half shells of Easter eggs.

- Chicken bone. Our church has good structure, but I prayed God would put flesh on the bones.

- Litter was down.

- Lots of balloons from water balloon fights that day.

- Prayed over picnic tables where the team going to pass out flyers was going to be.

- Prayed for Tommy and his family.

- Prayed over the events of the church via the TV.

Be Cautious

If you choose to pick up your prayer requests by gathering litter, please be careful. There are some items you should not pick up with your bare hands. Use tongs or gloves to pick up syringes, sharp items, or ones that might carry communicable diseases.

And there are places you probably shouldn't go alone or after dark. Use common sense, carry a cell phone, or go with a friend.

Preparation

Step One: Pray first

My first step is always to pray. It might sound odd to pray for prayer time, but try it. At the beginning of the week, during the week, and toward the end of the week, I'm praying for God to share His concerns and to lead me to pick up the trash that He wants me to lift up in prayer.

Step Two: Go to bed on time

If I want to walk on Saturday morning, I can't stay up late on Friday night. That's because if I'm tired, I'll be tempted to stay in bed where it's cozy and warm and then miss out on the time that God has prepared for us. I see prayer walking as my date with God.

Also, if I lay out what I'm planning to wear, it gets me out of the house faster. Select clothing that is loose and comfortable because you'll be bending over and moving a lot. If I don't lay the clothes out, I may wake my husband or daughters in search of a lost tennis shoe. If I awaken them, it often delays my walk even more because of a need they have. Also have a lightweight jacket handy in case you need it for breezy early morning walks.

In the winter months, I wear layers so I can take them off easily as I warm up.

Step Three: Don't forget the grocery bag

This has become such a big part of my walk. I have carried one with me for so long that now as I pick up prayers, it would feel a little strange not to have one. The bags are located in a drawer in my kitchen, so on my way out of the house, I just open the drawer, grab a sack, and tuck it into a pocket until I need it.

The only item I don't carry with me every time is a CD player. This is because movement causes it not to work or to skip sometimes. That frustrates me, so I concentrate on fixing it instead of spending time with God. I treasure this time so much that I don't want to waste one minute on anything unnecessary. So a new CD player—or an iPod—may be in order, although listening to music of any kind can be distracting for some. Figure out which way works best for you.

Step Four: Leave the dog at home

Sometimes, I have thought about taking Cody, my dog, with me, but I know Cody. He would stop every few feet with his never-ending sniffing. For me, it's better to leave him at home. I don't want anything to get in my way, distract me, or cause me to leave earlier than necessary. I want to make sure I'm up, ready, and "in tune" for God. Unless, of course, I could train Cody to sniff out the prayers God wants me to pray. But that's a topic for another book!

Walking

Step One: Take the first step

This can be the hardest part. On my way through the house, I see so many things that need to be done. I see dishes from the night before that didn't make it in the dishwasher and I see dirty clothes everywhere. I notice shoes and toys on the floor needing to be picked up. So… maybe I should add blinders to Preparation Step Three. I have learned to take a deep breath and say to myself, "It will be here when I return. It's okay. Keep walking toward the door."

Step Two: Soak in the quietness of the morning

Walking down the streets in my neighborhood, I'm always amazed at the beauty of the morning. It seems so fresh and clean, unmarked by the craziness of the day that is sure to come.

Praising God and offering thanks, I walk past homes, praying for neighbors. As I walk to the church, I ask God to show me any unconfessed sin in my life and as Psalm 51:10 says, "…renew a steadfast spirit within me." I don't want anything to block my communication with God. I want the Holy Spirit to be free to guide and direct me.

Step Three: Look for clues

On the edge of the property line, I say a simple prayer for the beginning of my prayer walk. It goes something like this:

Dear Heavenly Father, this morning I desire to honor and glorify Your name. I'm so excited for our time here together. What a beautiful morning that we get to spend in one accord! Open my eyes that I may see prayer requests and needs within my church family and my own family. Thank You for this time, and may Your will be done. In Jesus' precious name, amen.

After that prayer, I start my walk. Simply looking around, I begin praying for what I see. The church signage, the buildings, the playgrounds, ball field, tennis courts, landscaping, doorways—they're all fair game for inspiration. All the while, I'm looking for trash to throw away, as well as clues to use to pick up prayers. Because of the large size of our ten-acre campus, it's impossible for me to cover the entire area each week. I allow the Holy Spirit to guide me to the place of need. There's no pressure to walk the whole campus. I know what I don't get to this week I can cover the next.

For example, one week, I stayed around the back area. Walking around the gym, tennis courts, and ball field the entire time, I felt led to pray for the activities ministry and the week ahead. Later, I learned that the sports banquet had been held the Tuesday night after I prayed. It was the first time a direct salvation message had been delivered during the event. The reaction to the message was positive. So then, I knew why God wanted me to pray around the sports venues. God knew the desire of those preparing for the banquet and the prayers needed for a successful evening.

If possible, I walk around the main church buildings three times. To me, the three laps represent the trinity—God the Father, Jesus the Son, and the Holy Spirit.

Most weeks I pick up three bags of trash, again representing the trinity. Instead of bringing three bags with me, I simply empty one out in the trashcans placed around the property. As I dump a bag, I pray God will "throw away"—or forgive—our sins as we forgive others.

Step Four: Return home in gratitude

Leaving the campus, I pray like this:

Dear Lord, thank You for the time we had together this morning. It is so special to me. May You use me and this church during the weekend and the upcoming week to help others and to share with them Your love and devotion. In Jesus name, amen.

Walking toward home, I continue my conversation with God and ask Him for direction on my day, praying, "Father, what am I to do and where am I to go?" I want to be totally directed and guided by Him.

Step Five: Clean up

Usually when I get home, everyone is stirring, and the hubbub of the weekend is about to begin. However, before I give good morning hugs and kisses, I wash my hands with soap and water. I recommend that if you pick up trash like I do, try not to touch your face. In the winter, it's easy to wear gloves; and in the warmer months, you may choose to wear plastic gloves to protect you from germs. After washing up, I place one or two items I've found on the walk in a special box as a reminder of the day's prayers.

Two Frequently Asked Questions

1. How do you know what to pray for?

The words of a beloved hymn, written in 1912, come to mind. C. Austin Miles wrote "In the Garden," and one verse says, "He walks with me and He talks with me and He tells me I am His own." When I'm walking with God, He's talking to me and telling me I am His own. Because of that friendship, He guides me in what to pray.

> Call to me and I will answer you and tell you great and unsearchable things you do not know.

> Jeremiah 33:3

As I walk, I pray for God to inspire me and to give me thoughts on how to pray. Picking up an article of trash, I'll look at it and start asking questions, "God, what does this represent to the church or to me?" Then I ask questions concerning all senses: seeing, touching, hearing, smelling, and tasting. I don't actually taste any trash. But I do ask myself what it would have tasted like…bitter, sweet, cool, or hot, for example.

The most important step is being available, willing to take the time to walk. It's amazing what God will reveal to you when you concentrate.

2. How do you use the senses?

Here are a couple of examples:

- Hearing—The birds I hear when I sit on the bench in the courtyard remind me that just as God cares for the sparrows, He will watch out for those who feel like their lives are only worth discarding.

- Feeling—The breeze across my face reminds me of the Holy Spirit.

To give you an idea of how the senses and the prayer prompts come together, let me share an experience. One January morning, I spotted a marker. Putting it into my bag, I thought of older children and prayed for the Sunday school classrooms that would be filled the next day.

Around the playground, I picked up a pacifier. Not only did I pray for the infant it had belonged to, but I also prayed for all the babies in our church, "God, let them be raised in loving homes, growing up learning about Jesus and His love for them. Thank You, for the new baby room and the teachers added to the Sunday school program. This area of our church is multiplying!"

Walking toward the back of the campus, I spied an empty plastic bag. This struck me as funny because I admit...I had argued with God before leaving the house. Although I felt impressed to take another bag with me, I told myself it wasn't necessary. If there were a lot of trash, I would simply dump the contents of this bag out and continue on. But here in front of me was an empty bag. Sensing that I might need it, I tucked this one in my pocket.

Back by the children's building, underneath a bush, sat a small plastic toy man; he was only three inches tall. I wanted him for my prayer walking collection. What a fun item over which to pray. But there was a problem. I couldn't reach him. So I went off in search of a stick to pull him out. While looking for a stick, I ran across an empty oriental cookie wrapper, a plastic spoon, a dark crayon, and an unused ketchup packet. Finally, I found a long, thin piece of a tree branch.

As I walked back to the toy man, I noticed on the opposite end of the bushes another small plastic toy. I stooped down, and with the branch, pulled out the other toy. It was a lamb.

Suddenly, I knew God was giving me more than individual prayer requests. After retrieving the toy man, I went to a nearby bench and laid out my finds. The order came quickly:

- Black marker and dark crayon

- Baby pacifier

- Toy man

- Ketchup packet

- White toy lamb

- Plastic spoon

- Oriental cookie wrapper

My heart pounded as thoughts came to me about what each item represented.

The dark color in the marker and crayon could represent death, darkness, and sin. The marker and crayon could represent the type of mark we leave on others with our lives. With the pacifier, it was easy: What do we use to calm ourselves down when we feel angry, stressful, or anxious? Do we use an item that is colored with sin?

As for the toy man, he could represent us individually or corporately. And the lamb could represent sacrifice or Christ, the Lamb of God.

The red ketchup reminded me of the blood used to cleanse our sins. Ketchup is also used to flavor food.

The spoon is a utensil we use to feed ourselves. Because my husband, Richard, is an excellent cook, entertaining is one of our favorite things to do. Having people over to relax, converse, and visit is a comforting and fun time for all.

With the oriental cookie wrapper, I thought of the Chinese babysitter, Jenny, who took care of my children for years. She would give the girls Chinese treats packaged similar to this one when they left each day. The Chinese writing also reminded me that the world had come to my neighborhood. Where I live today, unlike the farm on which I grew up, my family is exposed to so many cultures. My daughter Kaitlyn has more than forty nationalities in her high school alone.

Here is an exercise for you! Reviewing the items, how would you pray?

_____

_____

_____

_____

_____

_____

_____

_____

Here's how I formulated my prayer:

The world (oriental cookie wrapper) without Jesus is in darkness and sin (crayon and marker). We (toy man) use many things to calm us down, to fill our time of boredom and to curb our appetites for things that are not good for us (pacifier).

But Jesus (toy lamb) can cleanse (packet of ketchup) us from our sins (crayon and marker) and call us to dine (plastic spoon) with Him. It's also a calling for people (toy man) who are believers in Christ (toy lamb) to confess their sin (crayon and marker) to release the strong holds (pacifier) and accept what Jesus (toy lamb) has done, and wants to do, for us (toy man). Until we confess (crayon and marker) and let go (pacifier), He (toy lamb) cannot send us into our community.

My actual prayer was: "Dear Lord, help me to live each day by spending time with You, releasing and letting go and allowing You to be in control."

I get so excited at the way the trash items come together that God must shake His head at me and say, "You asked Me to show Myself to you; you asked Me to reveal what to pray for. I did just that, so why are you surprised?"

It makes me stop and say, "You're right, of course, Lord. Thank You! I can't wait until next time!"

Putting all of the items from this prayer in the extra empty bag, I wondered if our new pastor had come to church for some reason. I was excited about how the items related together and wanted to share my prayer with him. In a fast walk, I turned toward the front of the church and stopped suddenly. In front of me, a dove sat on a bush by one of the entrances to the church parking lot. Not wanting it to fly away, I stood perfectly still and silently watched its movements and actions. The dove, a symbol for God and the Holy Spirit, moved its head back and forth, cooing softly. Within a couple of minutes, it left its spot on the bush and flew over the sanctuary. With all that had just transpired, I took this as a confirmation from God, telling me He was indeed present and desired to work and minister through all of our lives.

Silently I prayed, "Dear Lord, I thank You for revealing Yourself, the living God, to me this morning through the physical presence of a dove. I pray that we listen and hear Your voice so we, too, can fly with fluid movement in the direction that You desire us to go. Help us to hold on to the courage and hope that You give to us and to encourage each other in our walk with You. May Your Spirit continue to be active and working in our lives for Your glory. In Jesus' name."

Continuing around the main section of buildings, I could see that my pastor, Tommy, wasn't parked in the staff area, but that was okay. I just praised God and thanked Him again for what He shared with me on this Saturday morning prayer walk.

It's easier for me to figure out God's nudges when there's litter to pick up. But one particular Saturday, there wasn't much trash around, which was unusual. Though I normally filled at least three grocery bags, this day I simply walked around the church and asked God if there was anything special He wanted me to mention in prayer.

Trying to keep my eyes and ears open to His whispers, I felt the touch of a gentle soft breeze. It hadn't been there earlier. I asked the Lord, "Is this something to pray about?"

Feeling that the breeze represented the presence of the Holy Spirit, I prayed that He would enter into our church in a gentle way, and that He would be present in all areas: every ministry, every activity, and every heart.

· · · · ·

Prayer:

Oh, Holy Father: Thank You for making Your presence felt in small ways and big ways. Help us to always recognize the nudges and whispers that You give us. Help us to pray for all the people, places and ministries You want us to. And Lord, for people trying prayer walking or picking up prayers, please bless their efforts. In Jesus' name, amen.

Prayer Walk Your Church:

• • • • • • • • • • • • •

A CASE STUDY

As the popularity of prayer walking grows, more churches are holding group Prayer Walks, especially for significant events. Is your church launching a special campaign to do a helpful project in your community? Are you holding a Vacation Bible School? Is your leadership changing? Do you want to start a ministry? If you answered yes to any of these questions, consider joining with other members to prayer walk the grounds of the church. If you're just getting started, you might want to try the traditional Prayer Walk in which you simply walk and pray for the needs and concerns of the project, the church and so on. If you're more ambitious, try picking up prayers by selecting debris or using landmarks to guide your prayer time. With either method, the Prayer Walk will prepare hearts and minds; it will also seek God's blessings or answers.

Here's an example of a group Prayer Walk. In June 2006, David E. Crosby, pastor of First Baptist Church of New Orleans, sent an e-mail to invite members to prayer walk the day before construction began on forty new homes for families devastated by Hurricane Katrina.

Pastor Crosby began praying right in his e-mail.

Heavenly Father, watch over the building of these forty homes. May this project further the work of Christ in the city of New Orleans and may You receive all glory and honor for every good thing that takes place.

Let's talk about some tips for a successful group walk at your church.

Before The Day

Step One

Decide if your church's Prayer Walk will be outside or inside the facility or both. This could be dictated by weather, seasonal temperatures, or the prayer needs you anticipate.

Step Two

Prior to the date of the Prayer Walk, go over the area in which you plan to cover, actually walking the space and noting each area or landmark, such as the property line, playground, doors, landscaping, signage, parking lot, or cemetery.

As you walk, think about ways you could pray using the landmarks. If you have a large church with several buildings on the campus, providing a map is helpful when assigning areas for prayer. Even long-time members may not know every nook and cranny in the church.

Let's say one of your landmarks is a cemetery. You might pray for the families and friends who have recently experienced a loss. You could also pray that the hassles that sometimes erupt when a family closes an estate go smoothly. And you could pray for the financial, mental, and spiritual well-being of those left behind.

When it comes to the parking lot and signs, you might pray that visitors coming to your church for the first time will feel welcome. You could also pray that a friendly member helps them locate an appropriate Sunday school classroom or the worship center/sanctuary.

Inside the church, walk through every classroom, office, choir room, fellowship hall, and location of corporate worship then note what activities happen in each place throughout the year. Think beyond Sundays and Wednesdays. Consider such events as VBS, funerals, weddings, baptisms, baby dedications, and meals. Your church may also host civic groups such as Boy Scouts or Toastmasters. Some churches even become polling places on election day.

In the sanctuary, pray near the pulpit for the preacher and his Sunday sermons. In the choir loft, ask for the singers to be music worship leaders. In front of the baptismal pool, pray for new believers and their walk with the Lord. Sitting in the pews, pray for the worshippers to come with open hearts and minds to the messages they will hear.

You can go as deep and detailed as you want. For example, in each classroom, provide the names of teachers, helpers, students, their parents, and their siblings. In addition to the Prayer Walk, each teacher could pray on a weekly basis before coming into the classroom. Teachers could arrive early and pray for their classes, for each student to digest the lesson and apply it to their lives, and for the students' week ahead.

Step Three

Make an announcement about the Prayer Walk at least a month before it's to take place. Tell people where the walk will start and what time it begins. Nine in the morning is a good time to start. It's not too early and yet doesn't eat into the day too much.

Before deciding on the date, look at the church, local school, sports, and holiday schedules to ensure there are no obvious conflicts. Give assignments for at least two participants, but no more than four, to go together. More than four may slow the group in moving from area to area. You can either pray aloud, going around in the group, with each taking turns, or each person in the group may choose to pray silently.

I have even been in a group where all of us prayed aloud at the same time. That was powerful. All participants can learn from each other about how to pray. For more tips on recruiting others to join a Prayer Walk, see chapter ten.

Step Four

As mentioned in step two, create a guideline for the Prayer Walk. Depending on the size of your church, divide the church in sections, for the interior and exterior. For the first Prayer Walk at my church, I divided the areas by color like the Boston subway system that I used often as a newlywed. Each prayer walking area was identified by a color that represented its area:

- Blue Line: Offices, Library, Prayer room, and Chapel

- Purple Line: Babies, Children, and Adult Sunday school classrooms

- Green Line: Property Line, Signage, Landscaping, Playgrounds, and Facilities Staff

- Red Line: Main Sanctuary, Singles, College, and Youth Sunday school classes

- Orange Line: Choir Room, Fellowship Hall, Kitchen, and Dining Room

- Yellow Line: Activities Field, Gym, and Parking Lot

Trying to cover the entire campus of a large church could be overwhelming and impossible in the following time frame. So using the "divide and conquer" strategy, with each team taking a color, will make sure that all areas and ministries are covered in prayer.

Suggested time frame:

8:00–8:45 a.m.

1. Planning chief or committee arrives early to open the church building and make sure all doors are unlocked.

2. Pray for the morning.

3. As individuals arrive, pray silently for them, that God will use and impact their time for His glory and their own walk with Him.

8:45 - 9:00 a.m.

As walkers arrive, ask them to sign in. You want them to register so you can call or write to them later and thank them for participating. This time also provides a few minutes for fellowship.

9:00—9:10 a.m.

1. Start on time. People appreciate this and will more likely participate again if you show respect for their personal schedules.

2. Provide an introduction that includes a thank you for coming and a confirmation of why they are doing the Prayer Walk. It could be for an opening of a new building, general overall prayer for the church, upcoming events, or outreach and growth.

3. Before departing, have a group prayer for the walk. It works best if this is pre-assigned.

4. If you have not already assigned teams of two to four, now is the time to ask people to form partnerships with one to three other individuals. Be sensitive. Make sure no one is left out. You don't want anyone to feel like he or she is the last one picked, like in an elementary school kickball game. You may need to help form the groups.

5. Explain the plan and assign a territory to each group. You may want to provide a sample prayer for people who have never prayer walked before.

9:15–10:00 a.m.

6. Get them going! They are free to begin! Ask them to return forty-five minutes later.

7. Depending on the size of the group, have one or two people available for general questions during the walk time. These volunteers should be visible so participants don't have to use time hunting them down instead of praying.

10:00–10:15 a.m.

8. Have the group come back together for a period of sharing and celebrating what God put on their hearts. To help get this started, ask someone ahead of time to volunteer to speak first. This helps others join in.

9. Close in prayer.

10. After everyone has left, make notes on what worked and what needs improvement for the next walk.

11. Remember to write notes or call within the next three days to thank all of the walkers for their time, participation, and prayers.

12. Ask God when He wants you to have the next Prayer Walk!

If you meet resistance to holding a Prayer Walk or have few participants, don't be discouraged. That makes it easy to know what to pray about!

Your group may be like some of the dirt on my church's property. This dirt is exposed and very hard, while the shrubbery is prickly, shapeless, and scrawny. When anything needs to be picked up near the shrubs, I have to be careful because the bushes will stab me.

Many times, I've wondered what the dirt and the shrubs represent. Matthew Henry may have understood when he said, "Evidence of our hardness is that we are more concerned about our sufferings than our sins."

A couple of times, I've been caught in the rain, and the dirt is so hard that even a pounding rain does not penetrate the soil. It simply runs off. Does that ever happen to me or the church? Is God trying to speak to us, but our hearts are so hard that His message doesn't penetrate? Am I ever so vague and short with people—unapproachable like a thorn bush—that someone would be afraid to visit the church? When leaders are guiding us in a new direction, do we show our prickly side to try to prevent change?

Early in my prayer walking, I also noticed hard dirt in the medians located in the back parking lot. The medians have a tree or two planted in them with a skinny bush here or there, some dead, some alive. The lack of attention to the landscaping is probably the result of a lack of funds, construction at the church, or both. However, the hard dirt always caused me to pray with great concern for what it might represent. We got so used to the condition of the medians, that we no longer noticed how bad they looked.

So I prayed, "Dear Lord, please take away whatever causes our hardness of heart and spirit. Help the church and me not to turn our hearts against You. Keep our hearts repentant so we will not become hard, apathetic and blind toward Your Word. Let Your messages soak into our souls. Help us not to overlook any issues in our lives that need to be dug up and replanted. Help us not to be prickly to those looking for You or to those trying to show us a new way. In Jesus' name, amen."

In the spring of 2006, one Saturday night at midnight, I stood at the back of a large single room on the second floor of our church's gym (the location of our contemporary service) looking over the newly designed space. Emotions took over as I started to cry tears of relief and joy! We had made the tight deadline with the help of several volunteers. Richard and I had taken a utilitarian all-purpose room and transformed it into an attractive, relaxing space that would hold our new coffee house. The next morning, Easter, was going to be its grand opening.

Standing there, I felt God say, "Do you see how I used you, not only to pray for the space but also to design it?"

It hit me that I'd been praying for a place for members and their unchurched friends alike to come together in a nonthreatening environment to visit, hear, and discuss Jesus Christ. Our main problem was money; we didn't have enough to begin and complete this project. A group of us began praying for the funds to start this project. I even began seeing coffee cups on Saturday morning!

Our pastor, Tommy, wanted to bring the need before the congregation along with other future projects and had Tonya Roberts, the chairperson for the coffee house, talk to the church one Sunday morning about what the team wanted to do. A nonmember visiting family that day heard Tonya's plea and felt led to donate a large sum of money with the requirement that his or her name not be shared! We never dreamed God would finance the coffee house solely with one generous, anonymous gift from a person who wasn't even going to be drinking the java! God also answered prayers, beyond my imagination, concerning the shopping "deals" to furnish and decorate the area in a top notch way.

Used Starbucks® tables and chairs were located, and we received the opportunity to look at a large furniture distribution sale, an hour ahead of time, when an advertising flyer landed in our hands by mistake. It allowed us to get the nicest items. We also took out-of-the-box IKEA® kitchen cabinets and transformed them into a coffee bar. That alone saved hundreds of dollars. The list of miracles went on and on. During the entire process, we could see God's hand through every part of it, and that gave us the drive to finish on time.

Sunday morning was so full of God's Spirit that it was electrifying. It was fun to watch people's responses as they walked up the stairs and turned the corner. Mouths dropped open and faces appeared stunned. I even heard a few "Wow, it's over the top!" comments about the interior design. No one dreamed this formerly institutional-looking space could turn into a warm, comfortable

Starbucks® look-alike. I gave God all the glory for the design. Each step I took, I'd pray for God's guidance in design and furnishings. As I was working, it was if an angel would "sing" in my head when it was the right step to take or item to select.

The comparison is striking between what happens when you let "your designer" have full control of his or her ability to create a dream space for you and when you don't. It probably happens in other professions, too, between clients and vendors.

The interior design relationship is one of those that demands complete trust, even when construction is taking place and the area looks like it is in complete disarray with no end is in sight. Then it's done, and you have this incredible space! But what so often happens is the client gets nervous and starts questioning, makes changes and stops the process. The design and plan always suffer. So it is with God. He sometimes has to take us through periods of construction to shape, mold and create us into His ultimate, perfect plan. But we so often question, make changes, and stop the process because of the dust, confusion, and lack of trust in the designer.

It's like picking up trash to determine your prayers of the morning. Who would have ever dreamed that process would bless me and our church so much? What seems like a messy job has a perfect outcome. Prayer walkers who pick up trash have to trust the Lord.

· · · · ·

Prayer:

Gracious Father, You are the great and masterful Designer. Although it's difficult for us, help us to turn over control to You so You can complete the design for our lives and for our churches. Dear God, help us to never question Your plan, even when it seems the disarray and construction blind us from the vision, the vision that's often so much better than we could ever have imagined. In Your precious Son's name, amen.

Prayer Walk Your Home:

• • • • • • • • • • •

A GOOD PLACE TO START

Gray Temple, an Episcopal priest, is rector of St. Patrick's Church in Atlanta. He states in his book *When God Happens* that a wise friend told him,

> "God does not usually appear *during* your quiet time; God usually appears *because* of your quiet time." And there's an advantage to your regular time of prayer occurring first thing in the morning. What you do with your mind for the first half hour after waking sets the emotional tenor of the entire day. If you begin your day wishing for your heart to rub against the heart of God, you will live out the day with enhanced sensitivity to God's presence.[1]

That's my prayer for what will happen while I prayer walk on Saturday mornings. I so deeply desire for my heart to touch God's, for my day to be enhanced with His presence. But it's also a prayer we can say every morning—the moment we arise—that our family will be sensitive to God all day long.

Father Temple also mentions in his book that

Archbishop William Temple (no relation) was once asked his theology of prayer. "The one who asked the question braced himself for a lengthy learned answer. The Archbishop replied simply, 'When I pray, coincidences happen, when I don't pray, they don't happen.'"[2]

This has been so true in my own experience with prayer walking, and I hope you, too, will feel God's awe-inspiring power and love, with amazing stories and coincidences that only He could orchestrate. You may be concerned about picking up prayers because you don't belong to a church that's convenient or safe to walk around. The good news is you can still prayer walk.

And you don't even have to leave your home. Look at the interior and exterior of your house or apartment a little differently, and you can experience the blessings of praying and walking. Also, you don't have to do it alone; you can invite a friend to participate with you. Then the next week, you could pray at his or her house.

Starting with the outside of your house or apartment building, take a look around. Let your blinders down and truly observe and examine the surroundings. Notice the grass, the landscaping, the neatness, and the items on the ground or on the patio. Look at the projects started yet still unfinished (Okay, that one hurts me, too). Take each area individually and see where God leads you to pray. It may seem strange at first to prayer walk around the outside and inside of your home, but it will become easier with time.

Remember the statement coincidences happen when you pray? I want God to happen, and especially, I want

God to happen in my home. No other group of people is as dear to me as my family. Desire, determination, and mercy are in my prayers for God to bless them beyond measure. So "picking up prayers" in the home means noticing the little things that trigger thoughts, that trigger prayer needs for those you love the most.

The Lord has promised an abundant life for all who believe in Him. So praying for my own home is so much different from prayer walking around the church or neighborhood. There I pick up trash, pray, throw away, and let God take charge. At home, sure, we are picking up, but we don't forget about the items or just discard them like we do in other places. And it's harder to let God take charge, when our concerns, hurts and needs are so personal.

So that's why the home, I confess, is the hardest spot for me to pray. It's difficult for me to be so patient. Sometimes it seems like my prayers don't get answered fast enough or at all.

Still, prayer walking within my home has become such a tender and compassionate activity for me. Saying prayers has helped me to not get so stressed over the "clutter and mess" that occur within our home's walls. Instead, I now have the attitude—or perception of an opportunity—to pray and lift up the people I hold nearest to my heart. I hope my family has seen the "new me" instead of the mom on a warpath, complaining about the lack of help in picking up their things. Prayer walking has become to me, the best way to deal with, accept, and promote peace and love to each family member in all the areas of their hearts, souls, and minds. My prayer is for all to draw near to God, because He is waiting to draw near to them.

To help you get started on picking up prayers in your home, please consider the following categories: preparation, room-by-room observation, and general pick-up.

Preparation

1. Pull out your calendar or bring it up on the computer and create a schedule, including date and time on when and how long you are going to pray for each room, its occupant, and/or activities. Start with five to ten minutes per room.

2. Add it to your calendar. Otherwise, that time period will be too easily filled with a seemingly more urgent activity.

3. Consider prayer walking in your home right after your quiet time. That way your heart and mind are already in the right framework for more prayer.

Special Note: You can do one room a day or one room a week. What matters most is planning it out and sticking with it. You will be done in no time and then can start the process all over again. Be creative and have a different prayer theme each time. For example, each week you might focus on one of these: Blessings, Protection, Praise, and Thanksgiving.

Steps

1. Walk into the selected room.

2. Take a good look around.

3. Note the state that it is in: neat, orderly, messy, piles, no order at all.

4. Ask yourself, *What does this tell me?* and *How can I turn it into prayer?*

5. Begin by subdividing the room into activity spaces. As an example, the bedroom would have a sleeping area, but it may also have a study, dressing and/or sitting areas, too.

6. Begin praying for each area separately.

7. Once in that area, pick up one item at a time that you have decided to pray about, and while holding it, begin praying for the thoughts that are coming to you. Using your senses on each item, such as touch, can make it personal and customized. This action also puts the right tone on the situation. If you cannot pick an item up, simply touch it with your hand.

8. Move around the room and repeat the steps.

9. Before leaving the room, say an overall prayer for the person or persons who use the room, and ask God to cover them with His love and protection.

Room-by-Room Observation and General Pick-Up

As you "pick up prayers" in each room of the house, actually pick up items that need to be thrown or put away, and see if this leads you to pray. What works for me also helps clean the house! As I do each activity, I might pray for the child or my husband who touches the item. For instance, as I pick up my daughter's clothes, I offer a prayer of thankfulness that she is clothed like the lilies of the field that Jesus mentions in the book of Matthew. Or I might make a request that she will continue to dress modestly and be an example to her friends and classmates.

Here are a few room-by-room action steps that might inspire you to pray:

1. Master Bedroom:

    -   Strip bed of linens.

    -   Put out clean linens.

    -   Put clean clothes away.

    -   Put dirty clothes in the laundry hamper.

    -   Put kids' items that they left back in their rooms.

    -   Pick up drinking glasses to go back to the kitchen.

2. Master Bathroom

    -   Put away toiletries.

    -   Put dirty towels in hamper.

- Pick up toys from the nighttime bath and put back under the sink.

3. Children's Rooms

   - Pick up clothes, toys, books, towels, and drinking glasses.
   - Put items back on shelves, in closets and drawers or take downstairs.
   - Strip beds.
   - Put out clean linens.

4. Hall Bathroom

   - Pick up toiletries.
   - Pick up clothes and towels and put in washing pile.
   - Put clean towels on shelves.

5. Upstairs Office/Junk Room

   - Put books back on shelves.
   - Place paperwork in file folders.
   - Create a path.
   - Put items in here that do not have a home anywhere else.
   - Close the door.

6. Living Room

   - Pick up musical instruments and put in cases.

- Pick up sheet music and put in cabinet.
- Remove toys or projects that have been started and left.
- Put drinking glasses back in kitchen.

7. TV Room

- Remove wrappers from food items.
- Pick up magazines and put in a single pile.
- Put furniture back in place.
- Organize knickknacks on corner table and shelves.
- Pick up any garment that has been left on floor.

8. Guest Bedroom/Junk Room

- Clean off the beds that accumulate an unusual assortment of items.
- Locate homes for the items.
- Put unfinished school projects in here.
- Clean off the tops of the secretary and end table.

9. Dining Room

- Clean off the table, server and floor of items dropped when coming in from school or work.

10. Kitchen

- Load dishwasher.
- Wipe down counters.
- Pull out tools for cleaning service to use.
- Put clean dishes away.

Because many of the actions happen daily, when I needed to get out of the house for work, I would get frustrated. Feeling like no one was helping me created greater fury within me. I would reach out in prayer, "Lord, doesn't anyone see I need help? Lord, why don't they step in and say, 'Gee, Mom, I can see you could use some help. Let me.'? Is that unrealistic to expect or desire?" As silly as that may sound, it was my hope and wish.

The past process of picking up, putting back, or throwing away didn't change. What did change was the added element of prayer. As I go along now, doing the same things as before, I have a change of attitude and perspective.

Keeping the example of praying first as I do in my Saturday-morning prayer walks, I begin the same way here. "Dear Lord, here I am again, with the weekly clean-up chore. I pray for the right attitude as I go from room to room. May I see through Your eyes how to pray for each member of my family. Please show me areas of need and growth for the present and the future. In Jesus' name, amen."

A verse also helped me keep my temper in check, "Consider it pure joy, my brothers, whenever you face trials of many kinds, because you know that the testing of your faith develops perseverance. Perseverance must finish its work so that you may be mature and complete, not lacking anything" (James 1:2–4).

• • • • •

Prayer:

Dear Father, thank You for our homes. Help us to pray the prayers that will help our children and our husbands. Let us not get so concerned about cleaning and home maintenance that we forget to care. Thank You for answered prayers that reveal Your love and power. And help us not to get discouraged by the seemingly unanswered prayers. In Jesus' holy name, amen.

Prayer Walk Schools:

• • • • • • • • • •

THE REAL HEAD START

"Take a few minutes to stand by each student's desk and pray for that student, their family and their needs."

—Ellen Green, a Sylvia, Kansas, school principal who faces legal action for her National Day of Prayer memo to the teachers.[3]

You may not be a teacher who can pray out loud inside your classroom or a principal who can take an important stand. But just think about the positive impact you could have on our nation's future if you prayed around school campuses, preschools, and child care centers! You can pick up prayers at public or private schools—children everywhere need God's touch. You do not have to have a son or daughter in the school to pray at that campus.

You can pray for safety on the athletic fields and in buses. You can pray about the classes and the education needs. You can pray about the labs and tests, and you can pray that kids will be inspired to keep learning and achieving.

Here are some other ideas to lead you in prayer:

- Pray for teachers.
- Pray for administrators who have to make tough decisions.
- Pray for school board members who make policies.
- Pray for legislators to set fair funding for districts.
- Pray for those who write and edit textbooks.
- Pray for cafeteria workers.
- Pray for custodians and maintenance workers.
- Pray for parents.
- Pray for volunteers.
- Pray for the children's salvation.
- Pray for babysitters.
- Pray for coaches and referees.
- Pray for band directors, orchestra leaders and choir directors.
- Pray for the health and safety of all who walk on the campus.
- Pray for academic success.
- Pray for protection from violence.
- Pray for guardians, grandparents and foster parents.
- Pray that the students (and teachers) are shielded from temptation and evil.
- Pray for daycare center directors.

- Pray for parents who home school.
- Pray for boys and girls to have Christian role models.

Or you can pick up trash around the campus and see where the Lord leads you to pray. That happened to me one day. Underneath one of the bushes was a small plastic circle. Bending down and pulling it out of the pine straw, I immediately started turning it over in my hand. One side was blank while the other side had a smiley face on it. I realized it had come from the top of a cupcake that you would purchase in the grocery store for a birthday celebration. I remembered how my daughter, Kaitlyn, had this very same design on the top of her first birthday cupcake.

She had been at her babysitter's house sitting in the seat of honor (the high chair), watching me replace the smiling face decoration with a single candle. Her eyes became big when I lit the candle while her playmates, ranging in ages from two to four, started singing "Happy Birthday."

After the song was over, Kaitlyn blew out her candle and cheers erupted. Then, everyone received his or her cupcake and began to dig in. One child consumed the whole cupcake, while another ate only the cake and another licked off just the icing. Even though they ate their cakes differently, they all enjoyed the celebration.

After reminiscing, I began praying for the child whose birthday it had been, along with his or her classmates and also for God to bless them throughout the year.

Once again, I continued to turn the blue form over in my hand and looked at the smiley face. This time, questions came in my mind about how this could represent each of our faces to others at schools, churches, or in the community.

- *Do we reflect the peace that is beyond all understanding?*

- *Do we respond to situations differently or the same?*

- *Do we display the inner joy that is promised by Christ even though times might be tough or situations are beyond our control?*

These were hard questions to ask myself. They caused me to pray for our church that we would walk and express our faith, even in our facial expressions. And I prayed that school children would not know the tragedies that wipe off smiles, tragedies such as divorce, drug abuse, death, physical abuse, shootings, or hunger. But I also prayed that school children would know the joy and smiles that come with learning of Jesus' love.

• • • • •

Prayer:

Dear Lord, I pray for all of us and the birthdays that we have each year. May we stay like a one-year-old in the anticipation of the next year to come because we are spending it with You and doing Your will. May we reflect, respond and display the inner joy and peace that You promise to us to our family, friends and community. In Jesus' name, amen.

A month ago on my way to the church to prayer walk, I ended up cutting through the local elementary school yard. That morning I found a total of $2.50 from several locations. Can you imagine children setting down their change from lunch purchases so they could play on the playground or run around in the athletic field? After recess, they probably continued on their way while their handfuls of pennies, nickels, quarters, and dimes lay forgotten. If they were like my girls, their parents told them that morning to make sure they brought the change home.

I quickly prayed, "Dear Lord, if a child has forgotten her change, please don't let her parents get too angry. Dear Father, if a little one dropped his money, please don't let that be the cause of him going without a meal."

When I'm on my way to prayer walk at the church, I make it a point to look at the front lawn of the local elementary school, not for trash, but for what is posted on the sign. It gives me clues to what is happening at the school and what might need prayers. Even though my children are too old to attend it, the children and teachers are still of interest and concern. I don't know the gentleman personally who weekly changes out the messages, but I do know who he is. He is so creative and funny, I look forward to the new messages.

"Dear Lord, thank You for Lincoln's dad and the time and energy that he puts into this simple but powerful informational tool. Thank You that it is also a tool for me to use to know how to pray for the school. In Jesus' name, amen."

The sign has told me about fundraisers, picture day, and dinners at a local restaurant that give a percentage back to the school. One December, the sign announced the Holiday Performance. I said, "Dear Heavenly Father, I pray for the selection of the music that is to represent Christmas. May the music director select one that is about You and the baby Jesus that You sent to earth not to condemn us but to save us. Help me not get caught up in the craziness of the month, but remember the true reason for our celebration of Your Son. In Jesus' name, amen."

Coming back by the school on my way home, I walked on campus to zip through the back to a side street that also enables me to walk by more houses in my neighborhood. It was evident that the students were busy creating artwork because several windows had the masterpieces displayed. I prayed God would be with each of these children, that the love of learning be instilled in their hearts. I continued, "Father, may these kids listen to their teachers, and inspire the teachers to communicate the lesson to them in a clear and precise way."

Prayer "driving" by both the middle school and the high school has been the most effective way for me to pray for my girls' schools on a weekly basis. I am either dropping off Kaitlyn or Sarah and a project because it is too large to carry on the bus or I'm picking up after school to take them to an activity or doctor's appointment. As I watch them enter into the school, I leave with a silent prayer for their day.

Dear Heavenly Father, I thank You for Your presence with her today. Help her get her project into the school and settled in the right place without any trouble. Be with her during the presentation that she would be calm, collected and speak clearly with confidence on the subject that she has worked so hard on. Allow the teacher to find favor with her and grade her fairly. In Jesus' name, amen.

I also try to remember that each teacher has a family and stress, too. So often, I will pray for the teachers to recall why they got into their profession and experience the little joys of their jobs. I ask God for them to be treated fairly by their leaders and other parents, too.

• • • • •

Prayer:

Dear God, I know children are dear to You. Help us to help them with prayers for their campuses and their activities. May our communities' students learn well, compete heartily and be protected from those who might prey on them. Be with parents and be with all adults who can influence children to walk closer to You. In Jesus' name, amen.

Prayer Walk Neighborhoods:

• • • • • • • • • • • • • •

YOURS AND OTHERS

So, let's say you've tried picking up prayers at your church, around your home, and maybe even at a school campus. But you still feel you could make a difference with prayers in other areas. How about your neighborhood? These could be prayers that you say as you walk to the school or the church. You might pray for:

- The neighborhood's safety from violence, danger, and terrorism.

- Families to stay intact.

- Friendships to develop.

- Residents' relationship with Jesus.

- A spirit of community to grow.

When you think about the issues facing your own neighborhood, what prayer needs do you come up with?

_____

_____

_____

I was inspired to pray for my neighborhood one morning when I found an entry form for a contest to win a cruise. The form hadn't made it to the designated box, but instead it lay crumpled on the side of the street. The name on the card was a member of our youth group at church. This young man was one of my favorites and a member of the Sunday school class that I was co-teaching at the time.

He and his family had moved into our neighborhood and to our church within the past year. After praying that the family would feel accepted in the community and develop lifelong, affirming relationships, I prayed that the boy would become involved with the youth group and that he would grow in his spiritual walk with the Lord. Also, because he was attending a new high school, I prayed that he'd be an example to the athletic teams he belonged to, as well as to the rest of the student body. Unfortunately, he wouldn't be going on a free cruise for a week since I had his entry in my hand, but I did pray that he would accept the freedom that Christ had to offer him every day of his entire life.

Another Saturday, I found the section of the church parking lot near the children's building covered with discarded Kleenex. As I was picking up all of the tissues (with gloves on), I didn't think anything further about it, only that a virus must be going around.

But as I continued onto the parking lot near the place

of adult activities, I began to notice that the Kleenex were in this area as well. So, it dawned on me that the used tissues may have greater significance. Asking the Lord how I was supposed to pray, I felt there had been a funeral this past week in our neighborhood. Judging by the amount of tissues, the death must have filled family and friends with grief. I immediately started praying for those who had lost the loved one. Not knowing if this had been a sudden death or an illness that had lingered on, I did realize that the person who passed on had many friends who had loved him or her dearly. I lifted up the family left behind in prayer, asking that God would ease their pain and grief. I continued to lift up friends and any co-workers also feeling the loss of the person who had died. As I was finishing that morning, I thought of Lazarus when he had died and how Jesus wept. I felt He wept here, too.

Yet another day, walking along the side street that borders the church, I spied a pile of empty medicine bottles underneath a tree. Even though the bottles were all different sizes, none of them had any labels sharing the patient's name or prescription information. That wasn't a problem though because I believed God knew who these bottles had belonged to and why they were taking the medicine. Because God knows all, I started lifting the patient(s) up in prayer. One by one, I picked the bottles up to put in my plastic bag, and with each one, I prayed for the person's medical condition whether it was chronic, fatal or short-lived.

The older neighborhood near our church has original

homeowners still living in it, and because of the quantity of bottles, I speculated that they might've belonged to one of the elderly residents.

That led me to think how rural this area was forty years ago and how it is now considered metropolitan. Again, here is an example of how God knows all. He knew when a church plant had been started in a local elementary school that if its people were faithful, it would now be one of the largest churches inside what's called the "perimeter" of Atlanta. I thanked God for those founding members of my church and for their vision.

Could these pills belong to one of our long-term members or to a person who'd never set foot on this church campus? Once finished picking up the bottles, I continued walking to a new location and started lifting up the next item of concern. However, because of the medicine bottles, I have many times since remembered my church's start up and thanked God for our beginning, along with asking Him to bless our future.

• • • • •

Prayer:

Dear Lord, as time moves by so fast, we sometimes take for granted our health and development and the growth in our family, friends, neighborhood and even our church. May we continue to place all these in Your hands for Your will and purpose. Help us to continue to keep our eyes on eternal things that last forever and not on earthly things that fade away. In Your Son's name, amen.

• • • • •

During the night, our church campus is sometimes used by younger residents of the neighborhood. I can tell because of the items left behind. They're probably teenagers or young adults needing a place to hang out.

Unfortunately, they're not there to worship God or be in His presence. They seem to be there to hide and get away from the outside world.

The items they leave most often are beer bottles, cigarette packages, cigarette butts, and fast food bags. These items motivate me to pray for the individuals and the reasons they're there.

Once, I discovered how they stayed warm. They used shredded newspaper to start a fire and an old stew pot to contain it. The charred remnants of the newspaper remained in the bottom of the now blackened pot. From the number of items, it's usually only two or three people, not a large group—their form of a cell or home connection group.

In a way, I'm envious. When was the last time I came to church to hang out with my friends and just talk or reflect? I'm usually running fast, so I won't be late to teach a Sunday school class or attend a committee meeting.

Each time I come across a situation like the one of the night visitors, I ask God to give them a desire and a sense of courage to come to church during the day and for them to enter to drink from the living water. I pray for their education, parents, jobs, and most of all, their relationship with God. And, I pray for our church to have open arms to those who only feel comfortable coming on our campus at night.

• • • • •

Prayer:

Dear Father, please help our neighborhood to become a beacon for the city because of its love, its safety and its reliance on You. Bless the young and old who live in this community, as well as the families. Guide the Christians in the neighborhood to reach out to those who are seeking You and to those who might not know about You. Thank You for this neighborhood and all that it has meant to so many over the years. In Jesus' name, amen.

Prayer Walk Workplaces:

• • • • • • • • • • • •

EVERYWHERE IS ELIGIBLE

In most of our secular, corporate workplaces, we don't pray aloud for fear of offending people of different faith traditions. But there's no ban on silent prayer! During your lunch break or after work, choose to prayer walk your company.

You could walk the exterior or interior of your building and pray:

- For the safety of the employees.

- For the executives to make wise and compassionate decisions.

- For managers who are just starting out in leadership positions.

- For the productivity and integrity of workers.

- For the products or services being sold to help people.

- For the relationships among your vendors and customers.

- For employees to have growing faith.

- For the health and safety of the employees' families.

- For the quality of your work.

- That the employees have positive attitudes.

- That you will always be kind and Christ-like on the job.

- That God will lead you to coworkers who want to know more about your relationship with Christ.

Knowing the special challenges that face your organization, what might you pray as you walk around the company?

_____

_____

_____

_____

_____

_____

Workplace Definitions

Perhaps you don't work outside the home or you're retired. That doesn't mean your prayers for the workplace aren't needed. Think about how commerce affects your community. Successful corporations bring new families to town. Great restaurants give us choices about our meals. Nice retail shops provide opportunities to buy special gifts or to ask for sponsorships of worthwhile nonprofit activities.

When the economy is supported by thriving businesses, crime rates go down, domestic violence decreases and funding for good causes goes up.

So even if you or someone in your family is not directly employed in the workplace, please consider prayer walking your local businesses. Just think, some might call it window-shopping, but you can be prayer walking!

And remember people just don't work in offices or stores. They also work on the roads, in fields, at hospitals, on television, fighting fires, and chasing down criminals. Anyone earning a paycheck—or trying to earn one—could use our prayers.

Wanting Work

Let's also pray for the unemployed. If your family has known the pain of being downsized, laid off or otherwise being without work, you know how unemployment can affect marriages, kids, and self-esteem.

As a self-employed interior designer, if I have no clients, I have no work. One particular time, I specifically asked my mother to pray for my business. After ten years, due to a change in management, I lost my number one client. Literally, one day I was handling the design and furniture needs for ten medical centers, and the next day, I was thanked for many years of hard work and dedication.

The new management wanted to bring in another design firm that it had worked with at another company. I was heartbroken. This group had become more than a client; it had become a collection of good friends. I had separation anxiety from the loss of friendships and the loss of funds.

"Mom," I said to my mother in Indiana over the phone, "I need your prayers. Can you pray that God will bring another big account to replace the one I lost six months ago?" The timing had worked out fine. I was pregnant and this gave me the opportunity to slow down a bit for the delivery, but now I needed to get back to work.

A few weeks later, my parents were visiting and during their trip, I took my mother with me to a prayer conference. The speaker was Becky Tirabassi, and she was talking about developing your prayer life. Even though my mom could probably have taught the course, I thought she'd enjoy going with me. The event was held in a large downtown church where we used to be members. I was excited about the speaker and seeing some old friends, too.

At one of the breaks, I left to check the book table and catch up with friends. Mom decided she didn't want to go and would just stay in her seat. Another woman had decided to do the same. As everyone left, my mother and the other lady started talking. I returned to find my mother talking nonstop to her. The other lady was African-American and my mother is Caucasian. My heart jumped. I grew up in the beautiful farm land of Indiana where there are few black people. We had no past history of hurts or wrongs to reflect or dwell on. My heart stopped because just that weekend, my mother had asked a black lady in the grocery line if she could touch her hair. It felt like at that moment, everyone in the entire store stopped breathing. Sensing that my mother was not asking to humiliate her but that she truly wanted to know what her cornrows felt like, the woman bent over and allowed Mom to stroke her hair. Mom said, "Thank you," and the cashier continued checking us out. The store's activities began again.

So here I was, watching my mother talking to another lady who is African-American, hoping that in her innocence, Mom was doing nothing to offend this woman or tear down race relations in Atlanta. As I got closer, my mother turned to me and immediately said, "Valerie, I want you to meet my new friend, Lenora."

Lenora was a beautiful lady with a beautiful spirit. We didn't have much time to talk because the next session was beginning. The morning came to an end, and we all took away a life-changing message.

However, before we left, Mother and Lenora exchanged addresses and hugs. They actually started writing to each other. Mother would write about her life on the farm and activities at church while Lenora shared about her family and even some of her poetry.

During my phone conversations with Mom, she would encourage me to call Lenora and invite her to lunch. I kept putting Mom off. What did Lenora and I have in common aside from my mother? But finally, to get Mom to stop pestering me, I called Lenora, told her who I was and asked if she was available for lunch in the next couple of weeks. I teased her and said, "This way, my mother will stop mentioning it to both of us." Lenora just laughed, and we set our lunch date.

We had the best time! Not thinking anything about it, we met across the street from a large hospital. It turns out Lenora was the administrative assistant to the Director of Purchasing. She wanted to know what I did, and I told her I was an interior designer who also purchased and sold furniture, art, and accessories. She immediately told me that someone had that job at the hospital. I reassured her that I didn't come to this lunch to hunt down a new client; I just wanted to meet the lady my mother thought so highly of that she kept pushing me to invite her to lunch. Lenora and I both concluded that we were glad Mom pestered me.

About a month later, Lenora called, asking me if I had a brochure to send to her about my business. She explained that the hospital was now looking for a new "preferred small vendor" and would I be interested in coming in and talking with them? The purchasing director had mentioned the need to her, and she had remembered our lunch conversation. The appointment was set, and I arrived to talk to them. It was good to see Lenora again and to meet the director and the buyers. At the end of that first meeting, I ended up walking with Porcia Jones, one of the purchasing agents, to tackle my first assignment. I couldn't believe it all happened so quickly.

Needless to say, Mom was excited to see how God had used her to help me!

Soon after I started working with Crawford Long Hospital, I felt God leading me to do more than sell office furniture and artwork. He showed me I was there to pray. I felt led to begin in the emergency area. At that time, the loading dock was right next to the area where they brought in emergency patients. We'd have to wheel the furniture right by the ambulance area and through the same double doors. Seeing the needs, I prayed for the patients and doctors. So I wasn't picking up trash for ideas to pray. I was picking up ideas by looking at people!

When I saw patients come in without any friends or family members, my heart would go out to them. How alone and scared they must feel. I would pray for God to be with them and give them strength to hold on.

As I walked through the hospital corridors, I would see stretchers with patients being pushed to surgeries. I would pray for the skills of the surgeon and the success of the operation. Never before had I prayed about such life and death issues that were so close to me.

After a couple of years, I also was asked to call on Emory University Hospital. The one scene I will never forget happened while I was walking to an appointment. I glanced down the hall to see an individual bending over the seat of a wheelchair. It seemed as though he was experiencing a great deal of pain and grief because of a loved one who was in the hospital.

"Dear Lord," I prayed, "Please be with that person and give him comfort and strength to deal with the diagnosis."

In addition to praying for patients, I prayed for the doctors, nurses, and administrative employees in the areas for which I selected furniture. My experience with this hospital also changed how I looked at my other clients. Now, as I work with each, I ask God to give me clues through observations, conversations, and personal pictures on how I can pray for each of them. These prayers have changed my attitude about work. It's not a job; it's an assignment from God. He's placed me on site—on call—to minister to people both in their workplaces and in their personal lives. Most of the time, these people don't know I am praying. It's like being a spy for God.

Picking Up Prayers

Picking up litter on the grounds of a parking lot—company, church, school, or otherwise—can also lead you to pray for people in the workplace. For instance, while prayer walking at our church, I often find business cards. As I pick up the card, I begin praying for that individual and his or her work environment. I pray for the worker's and the company's success. Then, I pray that the person had a good worship experience at the church and that he or she will return again to learn more about Jesus.

Sometimes I wonder if I shared with folks that I pray for success when I find a business card, would more cards appear!

Picking Up Prayers in a Different Way

Maybe if you take a look at some of the items I've prayed over, it will give you thoughts and ideas of how you can pick up prayers at your job.

Start out with an overview prayer:

Thank You, Lord, for this project that has come my direction. Give me wisdom, insight, and knowledge on how to produce the best result/answer for it. May I stay focused and open to opportunities to share my faith through my words, deeds or actions. In Jesus' name, amen.

1. Building floor plans: Many times, I have prayed over a building plan and asked God to show me how to space plan. I can feel His inspiration on the design and layout of the walls and furniture placement.

2. Carpet Samples: "Lord, what direction do I go? I'm stuck. So many samples have come in that fit the specifications drawn up by the client. As I go through each one, give me the wisdom to separate. You are the master designer; allow my eyes to see the right one!"

3. Paint Selections: "Dear Lord, as I am pulling paints chips from the box, tune my eye to the colors that would be perfect for the main and accent colors. In Jesus' name, amen."

4. Furniture Samples being taken to the client for testing: "God, this is a big day for this client; final furniture decisions need to be made. Help me to show and demonstrate the best product for the task at hand while keeping in mind their budget."

5. Artwork: While searching through the bins for artwork, I keep in mind the approved color selections and the areas that need that final touch of art. "Heavenly Father, artwork can be inspirational, calming, and reflective and can bring a windowless room to life. Thank You for the artwork consultant who is helping me. Please guide and direct my search for the perfect selections that will produce the desired results."

In Others' Workplaces

My daughter Kaitlyn was taking a standardized test one Saturday morning south of Atlanta. We found the spot without any trouble and got her signed in. Because of the location, I decided to stay close by instead of driving back home.

Searching for a coffee shop that would allow me to settle in for the next three hours, I became frustrated, asking, "Doesn't this side of town like coffee?" Then I saw it—a combination flower/coffee shop. I eagerly went in. But the shop was empty, with no employees or customers in sight.

Walking around, looking at the prepared flower arrangements, I figured someone would come to the front. No one did, so not being shy; I searched in back and found two women working with the flowers. They jumped when they saw me. They'd been talking so much; they hadn't heard me come in.

Now laughing, one of the women left her current activity to see what I needed. Smiling, I said, "Coffee."

She brewed a pot, and when it was finished, she poured a cup of magnificent-smelling coffee. She told me to make myself at home and have all the coffee I wanted. So, I sat down at a large table by the window and started pulling out items from my bag. I wanted to work on notes for my Monday night Bible study. However, it turned out God had another goal in mind.

From my bag, I removed two Bibles—I like using different translations—a dictionary, colored pens, ruler, and notebook paper. Taking a sip of my coffee, enjoying its flavor and aroma, I began studying my lesson plan. After a while, the ladies came out of the back, bringing the flowers they had been working on for pickup. That's when I felt the curious stares.

Immediately I began to pray, "Lord, if You want me to talk to either of them about You, I am willing. Just send them over!" With that, I continued studying. But neither woman came over to me.

About an hour later, two men pulled up in a van. I soon learned through the conversations of the four workers that the two men were there to deliver the flowers. This had to be the main staple of the shop. Since I was the only coffee drinker that morning, java couldn't pay the bills.

Soon one of the men walked over to me. I didn't know what to think. Was he going to ask me to leave? He introduced himself as the owner and inquired about my daughter and her testing. I discovered one of the ladies had told him why I was sitting in his shop looking like I was planning on staying for awhile. He thanked me for stopping in and told me to stay as long as I needed. All the while he was talking, he was looking at my open Bibles. Finally, he asked me what I was doing. I explained I was working on the lesson for my Monday night Bible study. He wanted to know what I was teaching.

The main goal of the study was to teach women how to study the Bible and to lift each other up in prayer. He wanted to know more. I explained the easy method I learned from friends in college that I still use today. It opened up the Bible to me in a very personal way. He smiled and said he was a new believer whose pastor encouraged him to study and pray daily. He belonged to a small Baptist church in the area. He said he was having problems with his daily time with God.

His biggest challenge was a wandering mind. He admitted that during prayer, thousands of thoughts flooded his mind. They could be thoughts about his business, employees, current and future clients, or his daughter and all of her activities.

Guilt was eating him up with the thought that God must be disappointed in him for not being able to stay focused. He was also concerned he didn't have a ministry. He was praying for what God wanted him to do. Sensing that this man had a real heart for serving God, I told him what I'd learned just a few years earlier, *"Your work is your ministry."* God had him planted in this area (he had moved here to be close to his daughter, leaving a successful career as an attorney). He wanted to have more available time for his daughter, so he opened up this shop, which was close to her school, the location of Kaitlyn's test.

After my comment about his work being his ministry, he looked confused. I continued, "It's not just about making money to put in the bank to pay bills; it's also about seeing it through the eyes of Jesus. What would He have you do, what would He have you say, and who would He have you touch for His sake and glory? Think about your business. You bring people flowers. They're being sent to celebrate, remember, console, cheer, or add beauty to a space. As you deliver each flower arrangement, pray for the person or persons receiving them. They could be experiencing something that needs prayer. Also, pray for the people who come in for coffee or to purchase an arrangement to take with them. Make them feel welcome and show that you care. As they leave, silently say a prayer.

"Also, pray for your employees. You have probably learned a lot about each of them. Instead of trying to cram all your prayers in first thing in the morning, see your day as full of opportunities. The prayers don't have to be long, just one or two short sentences. God wants us to pray from the heart. Keep it simple."

Relief was showing on his face, and he was beginning to see that prayer could be an ongoing activity. Wanting to make sure he wasn't thinking about quitting his morning quiet time, I urged him not to stop trying to study the Bible. Martin Luther said his life was so busy he simply could not afford to miss his devotional time with the Lord each morning. He found that when he skipped this, his day was lost in distractions. I have heard over the years by several seasoned Christians that "Our hours stretch when we give reverence and time to God."

I also shared a little trick that I do. I keep a blank piece of paper close by me, and when a thought about work or family comes into my head, I simply write it down. That way, I won't keep repeating it in my head, afraid I might lose it. I explained to him that after his quiet time with God, he could turn his thoughts into his to-do list. This shop owner could also use the notes as a prayer guide for his day.

By then, it was time to go get Kaitlyn. Thanking him for allowing me to stay so long and for the pot of coffee, I left him with lots to think about. Driving the short distance to the testing site, I thanked God for the meeting that He had set up.

"Dear Lord, I just love sharing You with others. I lift this storeowner up to You and pray that he puts into action what we discussed. May You bless his business and his clients in every way. In Jesus' name, amen."

• • • • •

So, whether you pray for your workplace or pray in someone else's workplace, do pray. Hey, even those who work at churches need our prayers. And for that matter, so do those who work in the homes. The stay-at-home moms and dads may have the most important job of all—shaping the minds of the citizens who will be in charge one of these days.

• • • • •

Prayer:

Dear Lord, Thank You for the opportunity to work. Thank You for our jobs and for the jobs of our loved ones. Thank You for fulfilling work. Thank You for my coworkers and my clients. Thank You for the people who help us do our work, our suppliers and vendors. Thank You for those people who refer work to us and those who recommend us. Thank You for the good our company does in the community.

Please bless the leaders of our organization. Help them to be honorable and always do the right thing. Keep our company in business, so that no one will have to be laid off. Please help everyone to get along and put our customers' needs first.

Please keep workers in dangerous jobs safe. Bless firefighters, police officers, and emergency health professionals.

In Jesus' name, amen.

Picking Up People:

• • • • • • • • • •

ENLIST OTHERS TO PRAY

If you've been a churchgoer for a while, you've probably been asked to pray for others, either as part of the congregational audience, a Sunday school class, or Bible study group. You've probably noticed the "Prayer List" or "Prayer Concerns" section of the bulletin. You may even get or send prayer requests by email. You may take comfort in knowing that others are praying for you if you've ever made a request, and you may have observed the power of prayer when many people are petitioning God.

Earlier, I promised to tell you how to recruit others to prayer walk with you. Not everyone may like the idea of picking up prayers by picking up trash, so you can offer to be the picker-upper if that's an objection. There are many benefits to prayer walking and picking up prayers, so if you'd like a partner, try sharing these advantages:

•   It's good exercise.

•   It's good for the environment.

•   It makes our church/neighborhood/school campus look better.

- We can get to know each other better by hearing prayer concerns.
- We set an example for our family and friends by scheduling time for prayer.

Are there any other benefits to picking up prayers that you can think of?

_____

_____

_____

_____

_____

If you're recruiting for a Prayer Walk, you can ask for pulpit time to make an announcement. But there are additional, easy ways to let people know about an upcoming event.

- Ask teachers to announce it to their classes.
- Put colorful signs up in restroom stalls.
- Tape signs near trashcans, coffee machines, and water fountains.
- Write an announcement for the weekly bulletin or newsletter.
- Post an announcement on your church website.
- Send an announcement through email.

- Hand out empty trash bags with an announcement as people leave services.

- Have a sign up table decorated with trashcans in the lobby.

- Perform a funny skit for Ladies' Bible Class.

Perhaps you feel more comfortable picking up people to pray for instead of picking up trash. In addition to the individuals you know needing prayer, here are ideas of people to "pick up" in prayer:

- Lost individuals

- Members of the Armed Forces

- People in physical or emotional pain

- Caregivers

- Missionaries

- Our lawmakers and political leaders

- Single parents

- Learning-disabled children

- Physically or mentally challenged children

- People in low-income jobs

- Homeless people

- Widows and widowers

- Orphans

- Teenagers

- Homebound people

- Truck drivers who can't often attend church

What are other groups you can think of?

_____

_____

_____

_____

_____

Sometimes I find people to pray for in a store or even trying to catch a flight. It never ceases to amaze me how God orchestrates "divine appointments" in our daily lives. On a business trip to Michigan, the airline informed me of what would become the first of many delays. What should have taken four hours turned into ten!

Once in the air during the first flight of my stops, as the pilot announced the time the plane would be landing, I realized it was the same time my connecting flight was to lift off. I began praying, "What do I do? I don't know this airport. Could the next flight be delayed like this one? How will my luggage make it? Is there a reason for all of this?"

I hurriedly exited the plane and ran to catch the shuttle. I reached the gate only to find the seating area was empty with no airplane in sight. Learning I had already been assigned to a later flight, I shook my head and quietly let out a little laugh; I was going back to where I had originally landed!

Soon I realized I was not retracing my steps correctly. Somewhere I had taken a wrong turn. However, a sign indicated I could take an underground train to the next terminal. From there I would try to locate the needed shuttle. As the brightly lit train was pulling in, I noticed it was completely empty except for a young woman wiping her eyes as if she were crying. It was obvious she was trying desperately to get composed.

The train stopped, the automatic doors opened, and I felt drawn toward this woman. I stopped next to her. As she wiped her eyes again, I asked, "Is everything all right?"

She answered, "Yes, I'm fine."

"Can I help?"

She turned to me and admitted she'd just left the funeral service of her favorite student who was only fourteen years old. Aiding the family through support and the writing of the service, she commented that she had held it together before and during the funeral service, but now the sorrow was hitting her. While consoling her, I asked how the girl had died. The teenager's life had been taken by a mysterious virus that had settled in her spine. Thinking of my own fourteen-year-old daughter, my heart went out to this teacher and the girl's family.

The fast-moving train jolted to a stop and the doors opened. Now with both of us in a daze and saying a heartfelt goodbye, we started walking toward different escalators. She suddenly turned and almost in a shout, asked me, "Would you please pray for the family and for me?"

I assured her that I would. We both again turned and went in our opposite directions. Stunned with what had just taken place in a matter of a few minutes, the term "divine appointment" came to mind. God had set that meeting up; it was not by accident.

Upon realizing that, I proceeded and continued praying during the rest of my journey for the family and for the teacher who cared so deeply. I prayed, "Thank You, Lord, that I saw the divine appointment that You set for me and not the situation of missing my flight. It showed me how much You cared for the hurt this teacher and family were feeling and how You provided someone to pray for them. Continue to open my eyes to situations where Your love and prayers are needed."

Where I feel my prayers are most needed are with my family. One of my deepest prayer requests is that my children will walk daily with the Lord and that their faith will be deeply rooted and grounded in God's Word.

There's a saying that goes like this, "When they are little, you talk to them about Jesus. When they are older, you pray to Jesus about them." Looking back, I know my brother, Brad, and I have a close relationship with God today because of our parents' prayers. I don't ever remember hearing my mother tell me to read my Bible or to pray, but I do remember seeing her read her Bible and pray on a daily basis. Actions speak volumes. And it may be her example that led me to be open to something like praying over pieces of trash.

Throughout my life, I knew I could ask for prayer anytime, and Mom would add it to the top of her list. Nothing fancy, detailed, or long, simply a list of names that would be tucked into the side of her Bible, ready to be pulled out during her morning time with God for reading and praying. Once it was full, she would transfer the family names and other repeated requests to another page and start over. I do wish that she would have kept a journal with all of the answered prayers in it. Her sixty years of answered prayers would be inspiring. Her love for the church transferred to us, too. She was the church secretary for more than forty years, serving God faithfully week after week.

Early in my speaking career, I was asked to give my testimony at a weekend retreat. Once I got there, the stage seemed like the size of a city block, and there were more women of all ages than I dreamed of. I was beginning to get nervous. Why did I think I could do this? My heart was pounding to the point that I was sure others could hear it, and my adrenaline surged. I was hyperventilating. But I had to pray, "Dear Lord, please help me to calm down. I don't know how to stop these nerves."

To top it off, I'd told my mother to pray for me at a certain time, but the program was running ahead of schedule. I wasn't even going to get her help through prayer in this matter. That was the most upsetting thing to me that day because, over the years, I had come to rely on her prayers.

Right before I was to walk on stage, a feeling of peace came over me. I couldn't believe it. How did this happen?

I didn't have time to think about it because it was time for me to speak. I headed to the stage with confidence in what I felt led to talk about. The coordinator had asked me to share on a personal topic, but I had refused. Now I knew I must.

"Does anybody here remember the plate spinner on the Ed Sullivan Show?" I asked. Smiles came from the audience indicating they did remember and with fondness. I smiled with them and continued sharing how I feel like this Ed Sullivan act all the time. "Each of the plates is labeled with my different responsibilities—family, church activities, and work. I'm constantly placing a plate on a stick and spinning it, running to the next plate, spinning it again so it doesn't crash. Back to the first plate, spin, next plate, spin and so on. I thought I had enough plates, but God added one more to my life. The plate was called Monday night Bible study. Monday nights, I hold a Bible study for women interested in learning how to study the Bible through a simple method I learned in college. It was exciting to see women learn how they could take Scripture and study it for application in their own lives."

"God asked me to take the stick off another plate and lay that plate at His feet. The plate is called "depression." A few of my family members suffer from depression. I tried for a long period of time to keep their plates spinning along with my own. And Jesus said to me, 'Pick up the plate and give it to Me.' As much as I wanted to help by spinning it for them, I couldn't. The plate was going to crash, and I would blame myself. My part was to simply be available, loving, supportive, encouraging, and, most important, pray."

Unless you have experienced depression or know someone who has, it's difficult to understand the full dynamics, inner turmoil, and pain that overtake a depressed person. It's a helpless feeling for you and the person you love.

I finished my speech and sat down feeling totally drained and exhausted because I had not only shared from my heart but had exposed what the Christian world is afraid to talk about.

After the event finished, I was amazed at the people who came to me to talk about depression. Cynthia Clawson, the worship leader, was the first to reach me. She gave me a warm, supportive hug and admitted she'd been writing a song about depression. She'd felt God leading her to add something about "plates" to her song and didn't have a clue why. She said God showed her through my talk how to finish it. Next, a college student told me that her best friend in high school had committed suicide. The young woman told me she felt the family was too embarrassed to ask for help. She asked for continued prayers for all of them. Another woman told me about her husband and the never-ending dark cloud that surrounds him.

God showed me that day the need to open up and share about a topic that does not have to be crippling if all are willing to talk about it. That's the first step to recovery, talking about it and getting the needed help through counseling and proper medication.

Later that night, I called my mother and told her

about my talk. She wanted to hear all about it. Come to find out, her prayers were the reason for the sudden peace. God had impressed upon her to begin earlier and to go to her bedroom and get down on her knees in prayer. She didn't feel released until I was done. Mom had no idea that the time was not what we had talked about; she only followed the Holy Spirit's leading of, "Pray now!"

After our conversation ended, I prayed, "Dear Lord, thank You for my mother and her sensitivity to You and Your leading her to intercession for me. You knew how much I needed her prayers to talk about a potentially emotional and difficult subject that can cause uneasiness and discomfort. Let me leave this plate of depression with You and enable me to keep the others spinning with my eyes on You and not the plates."

While depression may not be the topic that you enlist others to pray about, you will have your own struggles. Whatever your challenge, know that the burden gets lighter when you ask others to pray with you, for you, or for your loved ones.

• • • • •

Prayer:

Heavenly Father, I ask for wisdom to know how to support and encourage my loved ones to a healthier tomorrow. In Jesus' name, amen.

Prayer Journal:

• • • • • • • •

YOUR TURN TO WRITE YOUR EXPERIENCES

It is my prayer that you are now excited about prayer! As you find the picking up prayer method that works best for you, I encourage you to journal your experiences or simply list what you pray about. It renews and energizes your faith when weeks, months, or years later, you look back over your journal and realize how God answered your prayers.

Here are some ideas to get you started. Organize your entries by:

- Date
- Place
- Location
- Type of building
- Room of house
- Items picked up
- People
- Topics

Now it is your turn! I pray that your relationship with the Lord will grow deeper as you journal and that you will find new and creative ways to talk with Him. To encourage you to record your own individual picked up prayers, here are pages left blank just for you to fill with your writing. God bless you with unexpected challenges, appointments, and tasks, which will draw you closer to Him!